November 20, 2003

To Jackie,

"I was a stranger and you
welcomed me."

Affectionately,
Lewis

ALSO BY HENRI COLE

The Visible Man
1998

The Look of Things
1995

The Zoo Wheel of Knowledge
1989

The Marble Queen
1986

Middle Earth

HENRI COLE

Middle Earth

FARRAR, STRAUS AND GIROUX / NEW YORK

Farrar, Straus and Giroux
19 Union Square West, New York 10003

Copyright © 2003 by Henri Cole
Distributed in Canada by Douglas & McIntyre Ltd.
Printed in the United States of America
First edition, 2003

Library of Congress Cataloging-in-Publication Data
Cole, Henri.
    Middle earth : poems / Henri Cole.— 1st ed.
        p. cm.
    ISBN 0-374-20881-6
    I. Title.

    PS3553.O4725 M53 2003
    811'.54—dc21
                                        2002029776

Designed by Quemadura

www.fsgbooks.com

10 9 8 7 6 5 4 3 2 1

For my teachers

Deadheading the geraniums, I see myself
as I am, almost naked in the heat,
trying to support a little universe
of blackening pinks, wilted by rain and sun,
stooping and quivering under my scissors
as I cut the rotten blossoms from the living,
as a man alone fills a void with words,
not to be consoling or point to what is good,
but to say something true that has body,
because it is proof of his existence.

Contents

I

II

III

·I

What high immortals do in mirth
Is life and death on Middle Earth

W. H. AUDEN,
"Under Which Lyre"

SELF-PORTRAIT

IN A GOLD KIMONO

Born, I was born.
                Tears represent how much my mother loves me,
shivering and steaming like a horse in rain.
                                My heart as innocent as Buddha's,
my name a Parisian bandleader's,
                                I am trying to stand.
Father is holding me and blowing in my ear,
                                like a glassblower on a flame.
Stars on his blue serge uniform flaunt a feeling
                                of formal precision and stoicism.
Growing, I am growing now,
                as straight as red pines in the low mountains.
Please don't leave, Grandmother Pearl.
                                I become distressed
watching the President's caisson.
                                We, we together move to the big house.
Shining, the sun is shining on my time line.
                                Tears, copper-hot tears,
spatter the house
                when Father is drunk, irate and boisterous.
The essence of self emerges
                shuttling between parents.

3

Noel, the wet nimbus of Noel's tongue

                       draws me out of the pit.

I drop acid with Rita.

            Chez Woo eros is released.

I eat sugar like a canary from a grown man's tongue.

                   The draft-card torn up;

the war lost.

         I cling like a cicada to the latticework of memory.

Mother: "I have memories, too.

                  Don't let me forget them."

Father: "I'm glad the journey is set.

               I'm glad I'm going."

Crows, the voices of crows

          leaving their nests at dawn, circle around,

as I sit in a gold kimono,

            feeling the subterranean magma flows,

the sultry air, the hand holding a pen,

              bending to write,

Thank you,

       Mother and Father, for creating me.

ICARUS BREATHING

Indestructible seabirds, black and white, leading and following;

semivisible mist, undulating, worming about the head;

rain starring the sea, tearing all over me;

our little boat, as in a Hokusai print, nudging closer

to Icarus (a humpback whale, not a foolish dead boy)

heaving against rough water; a voluminous inward grinding —

like a self breathing, but not a self — revivifying,

oxygenating the blood, making the blowhole move,

like a mouth silent against the decrees of fate: joy, grief,

desperation, triumph. Only God can obstruct them.

A big wave makes my feet slither. I feel like a baby,

bodiless and strange: a man is nothing if he is not changing.

Father, is that you breathing? Forgiveness is anathema to me.

I apologize. Knock me to the floor. Take me with you.

THE HARE

The hare does not belong to the rodents;

he is a species apart. Holding him firmly

against my chest, kissing his long white ears,

tasting earth on his fur and breath,

I am plunged into that white sustenance again,

where a long, fathomless calm emerges —

like a love that is futureless but binding

for a body on a gurney submerged in bright light,

as an orchard is submerged in lava —

while the hand of my brother, my companion

in nothingness, strokes our father,

but no power in the air touches us,

as one touches those one loves, as I

stroke a hare trembling in a box of straw.

POWDERED MILK

Come to the garden, you said,

and I went, hearing my voice inside

your throat. It was a way of self-forgetting.

Or it was a way of facing self,

I did not know.

        You drank scotch whiskey

and mixed me powdered milk,

as if I were still your boy.

Dogs tussled on the lawn around

Michelangelo's *David*, kept like a shrine;

big ordinary goldfish

chewed through the pond;

and the speech of bees encircled us,

filling a void.

A hundred blooming cacti

reminded me to be and not to seem.

When a squalid sky pulled down the sun,

we grew accustomed to it.

Darkness was no nemesis.

Come play checkers on the terrace,

you sighed.

Like me, you felt neglected,

you were in a mood of mental acuteness.

Like you, I was a man

with a taciturn spirit,

I was a man who would

never belong to anything.

Solitude had made us her illegitimate sons.

KAYAKS

Beyond the soggy garden, two kayaks

float across mild clear water. A red sun

stains the lake like colored glass. Day is stopping.

Everything I am feels distant or blank

as the opulent rays pass through me,

distant as action is from thought,

or language is from all things desirable

in the world, when it does not deliver

what it promises and pathos comes instead—

the same pathos I feel when I tell myself,

within or without valid structures of love:

I have been deceived, he is not what he seemed—

though the failure is not in the other,

but in me because I am tired, hurt or bitter.

PRESEPIO

This is the world God didn't create,

but an artist copying the original,

or some nostalgic idea of the original,

with Mary and Joseph, or statues of Mary and Joseph,

bowing their lamp-lit faces to the baby Jesus.

Language is not the human medium here,

where every eight minutes the seasons repeat themselves,

a rainbow appears, bleeding like an iris,

and the illusion of unity is achieved,

before blowing snow buries everything again.

Looked at from above, the farmer's sheep

are as big as conifers. Something is wrong with his sons,

whose pale bony necks make them look feral.

And the rooster cries more like a miserable donkey.

A light goes off. Another comes on.

In a little window, with a lamp to be read by,

nobody is reading. If God is around,

he seems ineffectual.

In the alps, a little trolley grinds its gears,

floating into the valley, where heavy droplets fall,

as the farmer's wife hurries —like a moving target

or a mind thinking —to unpin her laundry

from the wet white clothesline, and the farmer,

in the granary, stifles the little cries

of the neighbor girl parting her lips.

If the meaning of life is love, no one seems to be aware,

not even Mary and Joseph, exhausted with puffy eyes,

fleeing their dim golden crib.

CASABLANCA LILY

It has the odor of Mother leaving

when I was a boy. I watch the back

of her neck, wanting to cry, Come back. Come back!

So it is the smell of not saying what I feel,

of irrationality intruding

upon the orderly, of experience

seeking me out, though I do not want it to.

Unnaturally white with auburn anthers,

climbing the invisible ladder from birth

to death, it reveals the whole poignant

superstructure of itself without piety,

like Mother pushing a basket down

the grocery aisle, her pungent vital body

caught in the stranglehold of her mind.

MIDDLE EARTH

The soup boils over.
                    The doorbell rings.
The gas man demands payment for the last bill.
                              Can you find my yellow pills?
Mother interrupts meekly.
                         Fruit flies follow me, circling my head.
I drink wine to forget things.
                         I ride the train backwards.
I go to the zoo.
              I eat tiny marzipan men at the bakery;
desire and disgust get mixed up.
                         I read Kant:
stability is the fruit of both war and human insight.
                                        True or false:
more humans die as a result of prophets
                              than statesmen?
I scramble onto the ferry with Mother.
                    Iridescent ducks swim away like phrases.
Let me in, let me in!
                    I shout when I discern her child's face
peering through the dirty portal window.
                                   Look in my face,

I say like Frankenstein to his bride,

                         look in my face.

I repeat things in order to feel them,

                     craving what is no longer there.

The past dims like a great, tiered chandelier.

                        The present grows fragmentary

and rough:

            some days the visual field is abstract or empty —

in a windy sky, birds appear young and unwise;

                    others it's eerily concrete —

expressive figures move around

                 with an endless capacity for tumult

and uncertainty,

            taking us farther from ourselves,

into the aura

        at the deepest point of the river,

where grit blows in my face

            and my numb hands grip onto Mother's,

like love and hate

          in the shuttered mansion on the hill,

as red mist

      burns off the surface of the river.

VEIL

We were in your kitchen eating sherbet

to calm the fever of a summer day.

A bee scribbled its essence between us,

like a minimalist. A boy hoed manure

in the distance. The surgical cold of ice

made my head ache, then a veil was lifted.

Midday sprayed the little room with gold,

and I thought, Now I am awake. Now

freedom is lifting me out of the abyss

of coming and going in life without thinking,

which is the absence of freedom. Now I see

the still, black eyes saying, *Someone wants you,*

not me. Now nothing is hidden. Now,

water and soil are striving to be flesh.

SWANS

From above we must have looked like ordinary

tourists feeding winter swans, though it was

the grit of our father we flung hard

into the green water slapping against the pier,

where we stood soberly watching the ash float

or acquiesce and the swans, mooring themselves

against the little scrolls churned up out of the grave

by a motorboat throbbing in the distance.

What we had in common had been severed

from us. Like an umbrella in sand, I stood

rigidly apart—the wind flashing its needles

in air, the surf heavy, nebulous—remembering

a sunburned boy napping between hairy legs,

yellow jackets hovering over an empty basket.

RADIANT IVORY

After the death of my father, I locked

myself in my room, bored and animal-like.

The travel clock, the Johnnie Walker bottle,

the parrot tulips — everything possessed his face,

chaste and obscure. Snow and rain battered the air

white, insane, slathery. Nothing poured

out of me except sensibility, dilated.

It was as if I were *sub*-born — preverbal,

truculent, pure — with hard ivory arms

reaching out into a dark and crowded space,

illuminated like a perforated silver box

or a little room in which glowing cigarettes

came and went, like souls losing magnitude,

but none with the battered hand I knew.

APE HOUSE, BERLIN ZOO

Are the lost like this,
living not like a plant, an inch to drink each week,
but like the grass snake under it,
gorging itself before a famine?
Gazing at me longer than any human has in a long time,
you are my closest relative in thousands of miles.
When your soul looks out through your eyes,
looking at me looking at you, what does it see?
Like you, I was born in the East;
my arms are too long and my spine bowed;
I eat leaves, fruits and roots; I curl up when I sleep; I live alone.
As your mother once cradled you, mine cradled me,
pushing her nipple between my gums.
Here, where time crawls forward, too slow for human eyes,
neither of us rushes into the future,
since the future means living with a self
that has fed on the squalor that is here.
I cannot tell which of us absorbs the other more;
I am free but you are not,
if freedom means traveling long distances to avoid boredom.
When a child shakes his dirty fist in your face,
making a cry like a buck at rutting time,

you are not impressed. Indolence has made you philosophical.
From where I stand, you are beautiful and ugly at once,
    like a weed or a human.
We are children meeting for the first time,
each standing in the other's light.
Instruments of darkness have not yet told us truths;
love has not yet made us jealous or cruel,
though it has made us look like one another.
It is understood that part of me lives in you,
or is it the reverse, as it was with my father,
before all of him went into a pint of ash?
Sitting in a miasma of excrement and straw,
combing aside hair matted on your ass,
picking an insect from your breast, chewing a plant bulb,
why are you not appalled by my perfect teeth
and scrupulous dress? How did you lose what God gave you?
Bowing to his unappealable judgment, do you feel a lack?
Nakedness, isolation, bare inanity: these are the soil
and entanglement of actual living.
There are no more elegant redemptive plots.
Roaming about the ape house, I cannot tell which of us,
with naked, painful eyes, is shielded behind Plexiglas.

How can it be that we were not once a family
and now we've come apart? How can it be that it was Adam
who brought death into the world?
Roaming about the ape house, I am sweat and contemplation
    and breath.
I am active and passive, darkness and light, chaste and corrupt.
I am martyr to nothing. I am rejected by nothing.
All the bloated clottings of a life—family disputes,
    lost inheritances,
vulgar lies, festering love, ungovernable passion, hope wrecked—
bleed out of the mind. Pondering you,
as you chew on a raw onion and ponder me,
I am myself as a boy, showering with my father, learning not
    to be afraid,
spitting mouthfuls of water into the face of the loved one,
the only thing to suffer for.

I I

Wild air, world-mothering air,
Nestling me everywhere

GERARD MANLEY HOPKINS,
"The Blessed Virgin compared to the Air we Breathe"

BLACK CAMELLIA

[AFTER PETRARCH]

Little room, with four and a half tatami mats

and sliding paper doors, that used to be

a white, translucent place to live in refined poverty,

what are you now but scalding water in a bath?

Little mattress, that used to fold around me

at sunrise as unfinished dreams were fading,

what are you now but a blood-red palanquin

of plucked feathers and silk airing in the sun?

Weeding the garden, paring a turnip, drinking tea

for want of wine, I flee from my secret love

and from my mind's worm — This is a poem.

Is this a table? No, this is a poem. Am I a girl? —

seeking out the meat-hook crowd I once loathed,

I'm so afraid to find myself alone.

LANDSCAPE WITH
DEER AND FIGURE

If you listen, you can hear them chewing

before you see them standing or sitting —

with slim legs and branching antlers —

eating together like children, or the souls

of children, no one animal his own,

as I am my own, watching them watch me,

feeling a fever mount in my forehead,

where all that I am is borne and is effaced

by a herd of deer gathered in the meadow —

like brown ink splashed on rice paper —

abstract, exalted, revealing the eternal harmony,

for only five or six moments, of obligation to family

manifested with such frightful clarity and beauty

it quells the blur of human feeling.

GREEN SHADE

[NARA DEER PARK]

With my head on his spotted back

and his head on the grass—a little bored

with the quiet motion of life

and a cluster of mosquitoes making

hot black dunes in the air—we slept

with the smell of his fur engulfing us.

It was as if my dominant functions were gazing

and dreaming in a field of semiwild deer.

It was as if I could dream what I wanted,

and what I wanted was to long for nothing—

no facts, no reasons—never to say again,

"I want to be like him," and to lie instead

in the hollow deep grass—without esteem or riches—

gazing into the big, lacquer black eyes of a deer.

KYUSHU HYDRANGEA

Some might say there are too many

for a charity hospital, too many pale

pink blossoms opening into creamy

paler ones, just when everything else

is dying in the garden. They can't see

the huge, upright panicles correspond

to something else, something not external at all,

but its complement, that atmosphere of pure

unambiguous light burning inwardly,

not in self-regard but in self-forgetting;

they can't see the lush rainy-season flowers,

with feet planted partially in rock,

lifting their big solemn heads over

the verdant wounded hands of the leaves.

CROWS IN EVENING GLOW

The terrible glorious crows are convening again,

swooping into the area with triumphant caws,

plunging with demon black wings from utility poles,

kicking and pecking a neighbor's kittens.

Wearing the plaid shirt that was my father's plaid shirt,

I throw a tarp over a pile of clear pink

hemorrhaging garbage bags. See a crow,

take three steps back. Three crows cried,

someone has died. Go home, Crows! I holler,

My black-lipped daddy is gone. Poor crows,

perplexing as men, nobody is listening

to their tired signals, not even the mother,

with blue drooping breast, nursing a newborn

under a red maple with a nest.

NECESSARY AND IMPOSSIBLE

It is a nation born in the quiet part of the mind,

that has no fantasy of omnipotence,

no God but nature, no net of one vow,

no dark corner of the poor, no fugue-work of hate,

no hierarchies of strength, knowledge or love,

no impure water spasming from rock, no swarm of polluted flies,

no ash-heap of concrete, gypsum and glass,

no false mercy or truths buried in excrement;

and in this nation of men and women,

no face in the mirror reflecting more darkness

than light, more strife than love, no more strife

than in my hands now, as I sit on a rock,

tearing up bread for red and white carp

pushing out of their element into mine.

CLEANING THE ELEPHANT

Thirsty and pale, her face lowered in concentration,

she doesn't seem to mind my sweeping

insects and dung from her corrugated flesh,

permitting me even to brush her soft hairy nape,

where I dream of squatting barefoot one day,

like a figure in a scroll, to feel the immutable

place of thought, if an elephant has thought.

"What is the smell of being human?" I want to ask,

like Plato, desiring to witness the truth

as both elephant and embodiment,

pushing out everything else—as when a soul,

finding its peculiar other, pushes out

the staple of life, which is suffering,

and a red sun wraps everything in gold.

MORNING GLORY

Out my window, in a garden the size of an urn,

a morning glory is climbing toward me.

It is five a.m. on the ninth day of the seventh month.

Lying on my soft mats, like a long white rabbit,

I can feel the purifying flames of summer

denuding the landscape, not of birds and animals,

but of blame and illusion. I can hear the white

splashing rivers of forgetfulness and oblivion

soaking me all at once, like loving a man

without wanting him, or a baby emerging

under white light out of its mother,

not the artificial light of the hospital corridor

but of joy growing wild in the garden, its pallid blue

trumpets piercing a brocade of red leaves.

MYSELF WITH CATS

Hanging out the wash, I visit the cats.

"I don't belong to nobody," Yang insists vulgarly.

"Yang," I reply, "you don't know nothing."

Yin, an orange tabby, agrees

but puts kindness ahead of rigid truth.

I admire her but wish she wouldn't idolize

the one who bullies her. I once did that.

Her silence speaks needles when Yang thrusts

his ugly tortoiseshell body against hers,

sprawled in my cosmos. "Really, I don't mind,"

she purrs — her eyes horizontal, her mouth

an Ionian smile, her legs crossed nobly

in front of her, a model of cat Nirvana —

"withholding his affection, he made me stronger."

PILLOWCASE WITH

PRAYING MANTIS

I found a praying mantis on my pillow.

"What are you praying for?" I asked. "Can you pray

for my father's soul, grasping after Mother?"

Swaying back and forth, mimicking the color

of my sheets, raising her head like a dragon's,

she seemed to view me with deep feeling, as if I were

St. Sebastian bound to a Corinthian column

instead of just Henri lying around reading.

I envied her crisp linearity, as she galloped

slow motion onto my chest, but then she started

mimicking me, lifting her arms in an attitude

of a scholar thinking or romantic suffering.

"Stop!" I sighed, and she did, flying in a wide arc,

like a tiny god-horse hunting for her throne room.

MELON AND INSECTS

Pedaling home at twilight, I collided

with a red dragonfly, whose tiny boneless

body was thrown into my bicycle-basket.

In my bed, in a pocket notebook, I made

a drawing, then cried, "Wake up, Dragonfly.

Don't die!" I was sitting half-naked

in the humidity, my pen in my hot palm.

I was smiling at Dragonfly, but getting angry.

So I put him in a rice bowl, with some melon

and swept-up corpses of mosquitoes,

where he shone like a big broken earring,

his terrified eyes gleaming like little suns,

making me exhausted, lonely like that,

before sleep, waiting to show my drawing.

INSOMNIA

At night by lamplight certain insects,

floating or flying, in black or red or gold,

emerge like actors, vaguely apparitional,

in the ordinary space of my room.

Last night, they did *The Tempest* in a frenzy,

demanding I play Prospero and forgive

everyone. "What is this!" I moaned.

Dear unnatural Ariel, I loved him,

the island setting, the auspicious revenge —

how could I resist? The rain came down,

filling up time like sand or human understanding.

It was as if I were dreaming or dead.

I forgave my brother; he forgave me.

We huddled together in the dark backward of the night.

ORIGINAL FACE

Some mornings I wake up kicking like a frog.

My thighs ache from going nowhere all night.

I get up—tailless, smooth-skinned, eyes protruding—

and scrub around for my original face.

It is good I am dreaming, I say to myself.

The real characters and events would hurt me.

The real lying, shame and envy would turn

even a pleasure-loving man into a stone.

Instead, my plain human flesh wakes up

and gazes out at real sparrows skimming the luminous

wet rooftops at the base of a mountain.

No splayed breasts, no glaring teeth, appear before me.

Only the ivory hands of morning touching

the real face in the real mirror on my bureau.

MASK

I tied a paper mask onto my face,

my lips almost inside its small red mouth.

Turning my head to the left, to the right,

I looked like someone I once knew, or was,

with straight white teeth and boyish bangs.

My ordinary life had come as far as it would,

like a silver arrow hitting cypress.

Know your place or you'll rue it, I sighed

to the mirror. To succeed, I'd done things

I hated; to be loved, I'd competed promiscuously:

my essence seemed to boil down to only this.

Then I saw my own hazel irises float up,

like eggs clinging to a water plant,

seamless and clear, in an empty, pondlike face.

III

I hate and I love. And if you ask me how,
I do not know: I only feel it, and I'm torn in two.

GAIUS VALERIUS CATULLUS, #85
tr. Peter Whigham

MY TEA CEREMONY

Oh, you bowls, don't tell the others I drink

my liquor out of you. I want a feeling of beauty

to surround the plainest facts of my life.

Sitting on my bare heels, making a formal bow,

I want an atmosphere of gentleness to drive

out the squalor of everyday existence

in a little passive house surrounded

by black rocks and gray gravel.

Half-cerebral, half-sensual, I want to hear

the water murmuring in the kettle

and to see the spider, green as jade,

remaining aloof on the wall.

                        Heart, unquiet thing,

I don't want to hate anymore. I want love

to trample through my arms again.

SELF-PORTRAIT

AS THE RED PRINCESS

When the curtain rises,
   I appear in a red kimono, opening a paper umbrella.
Tucking my elbows into my waist,
     concealing my hands within my sleeves,
I circle the bare stage with tiny steps,
      holding my knees inward,
to create the impression I am small,
     because to be beautiful is to be small,
not young. I end in a dance of tears,
     placing my hand in a simple gesture
in front of my perfect oval face,
     indicating a woman's grief;
I am, after all, a woman,
    and not a man playing a woman.
Even with my mouth painted holly berry red
    and my waxed brows drawn higher,
there is nothing grotesque or cruel
    about my whitened, made-up face.
"The flower of verisimilitude," they call me —
     with my hair done up in a knot
of silver ornaments and lacquered wood
     and with my small melon seed face

filled with carnal love —
                         though some nights sitting for hours
with my numb legs folded under me,
                         pretending I have fallen out of love,
I cannot believe I am refining feminine beauty
                         to a level unsurpassed in life.
Bathing with my lover,
                         gazing at his firm stomach covered by hair,
pressing my burning face there,
                         and, later, dashing to freedom in the black pines,
I see that I am veering toward destruction,
                         instead of the unity of form and feeling;
I see a dimly shining instrument
                         opening the soft meat of our throats.
Feeding and mating we share with the animals,
                         but volition is ours alone.
Had I not followed a man to death,
                         I think I would have died quietly,
as I had lived.

FISH AND WATERGRASS

My heart and my body were separate,

when I got off my bike, soaked with sweat,

and put my face in the river, an ethereal

dark place full of algae and watergrass.

Unable to keep a tight control over

their coal-black bodies in the current,

a cluster of koi groped forward,

with white, translucent, overworked eyes

searching for something, as a man searches

after going a great distance.

                        Who were you

that even now all of me is in tatters,

aching to touch your face floating in dream,

defining itself, like a large white

flower, by separation from me?

AT THE GRAVE OF

ELIZABETH BISHOP

I, detaching myself from the human I, Henri,

without thick eyeglasses or rubberized white skin,

stretched out like a sinewy cat in the brown grass

to see what I felt, wrapping my tail around me,

hiding my eyes.

                I slept. I waited. I sucked air,

instead of milk. I listened to pigeons murmuring.

Scratching my ear, I couldn't tell if I was male or female.

The bundled energy of my life drifted along

somewhere between pain and pleasure,

until a deerfly launched an attack

and anger, like a florist's scissors,

pinched the bright chrysanthemum of my brain.

Overhead, the long enfolding branches,

weighted down with Venetian green,

suffused the air with possibility.

I felt like a realist, recovering from style.

Grief and dignity swirled around discreetly,

transferring to me an aura of calm,

as I lay in a shawl of gold light,

licking my paws, licking my throat,

my smooth imperturbable face revealing nothing,

even when I thought about my first loves,

surface and symbol, rubbing against me,

humping in the shadows, making my whole body tremble.

I purred, watching an iridescent blue beetle

imbibe chlorophyll from a leaf.

I flared my nostrils, hearing a starling

splash in an amphora of rainwater.

With my paws in the air, exposing my ripe belly,

I rubbed my spine, a little drunk on the ultraviolet rays

and on myself, I confess.

Then the sky cleared. Birds were flying.

I felt a deep throbbing, as from a distant factory,

binding me to others, a faint battering of wings against glass

that was the heart in the lovely dark behind my breast,

as I was crouching to tie my shoelaces,

feeling strange in the meaty halves of my buttocks,

until I sprinkled a little earth on my head,

like Hadrian reunited with the place he loved.

OLYMPIA

Tired, hungry, hot, I climbed the steep slope

to town, a sultry, watery place, crawling with insects

and birds.

      In the semidarkness of the mountain,

small things loomed large: a donkey urinating on a palm;

a salt-and-saliva-stained boy riding on his mother's back;

a shy roaming black Adam. I was walking on an edge.

The moments fused into one crystalline rock,

like ice in a champagne bucket. Time was plunging forward,

like dolphins scissoring open water or like me,

following Jenny's flippers down to see the coral reef,

where the color of sand, sea and sky merged,

and it was as if that was all God wanted:

not a wife, a house or a position,

but a self, like a needle, pushing in a vein.

MEDUSA

A vulture rose and flapped across the sand

as we approached. At the lookout, others

perched stiffly, like little martyred saints, with gaudy

red heads. It was too hot and I wanted

to go home. Soaring on thermals everywhere,

wood storks conveyed their own way of being,

not debunking violence, but commingling with it,

as if freedom meant proximity to danger.

When I poked the wet, mahogany mud,

it felt like something human I had my hand on,

as if the earth were a girl's black-haired head

being lifted up in a great clatter that ebbed

and flowed, like sea foam or a red sky or pain

obscuring pleasure in a flesh tunnel.

SNOW MOON FLOWER

In this place of rice fields,

metrical mountains and little bubbling canals,

it was not the self against time

or the self blurred by flesh, it was the self

living without any palpable design.

Common egrets floated on broad bowed wings.

A rooster crowed at dawn and the body—

graceful, alert—slanted gently toward the sun.

In the night gloom, a ground spider jumped

around the shortwave radio

on which a samisen played,

and fawnlike creatures ventured out of the pines,

observing in my windows a solitude

as pure as a bowl of milk.

But outside the gate of this place,

there was another mirror world,

connected only by a dark path of sticky stones,

where there were goat smells and little cries,

hooves pawing and flying beetles. No man could resist it.

No man could endure it. The long shadows

fell on the mind like nails in a plank,

taking one beyond the surface of things,

into the deepest places, not of man's griefs

but of man's truths, which cut deep,

if they did not tear us apart, like a field of thorn,

as the dark tops of the trees shone complacently

and a changing light filtered and breathed

against the lonely surface of everything.

BLUR

1

It was a Christian idea, sacrificing

oneself to attain the object of one's desire.

I was weak and he was like opium to me,

so present and forceful. I believed I saw myself

through him, as if in a bucket being drawn

up a well, cold and brown as tea.

My horse was wet all that summer.

I pushed him, he pushed me back — proud, lonely,

disappointed — until I rode him,

or he rode me, in tight embrace, and life went on.

I lay whole nights — listless, sighing, gleaming

like a tendril on a tree — withdrawn

into some desiccated realm of beauty.

The hand desired, but the heart refrained.

2

The strong sad ritual between us could not be broken:

the empathetic greeting; the apologies

and reproaches; the narrow bed of his flesh;

the fear of being shown whole in the mirror

of another's fragmentation; the climbing on;

the unambiguous freedom born of submission;

the head, like a rock, hefted on and off moist earth;

the rough language; the impermeable core

of one's being made permeable; the black hair

and shining eyes; and afterward, the marrowy

emissions, the gasping made liquid; the torso,

like pale clay or a plank, being dropped;

the small confessional remarks that inscribe

the soul; the indolence; the being alone.

3

Then everything decanted and modulated,

as it did in a horse's eye, and the self—

pure, classical, like a figure carved from stone—

was something broken off again.

Two ways of being: one, seamless

saturated color (not a bead of sweat),

pure virtuosity, bolts of it; the other,

raw and unsocialized, "an opera of impurity,"

like super-real sunlight on a bruise.

I didn't want to have to choose.

It didn't matter anymore what was true

and what was not. Experience was not facts,

but uncertainty. Experience was not events,

but feelings, which I would overcome.

4

Waking hungry for flesh, stalking flesh

no matter where—in the dunes, at the Pantheon,

in the Tuileries, at the White Party—

cursing and fumbling with flesh, smelling flesh,

clutching flesh, sucking violently on flesh,

cleaning up flesh, smiling at flesh, running away

from flesh, and later loathing flesh,

half of me was shattered, half was not,

like a mosaic shaken down by earthquake.

All the things I loved—a horse, a wristwatch,

a hall mirror—and all the things I endeavored to be—

truthful, empathetic, funny—presupposed

a sense of self locked up in a sphere,

which would never be known to anyone.

5

Running, lifting, skipping rope at the gym,

I was a man like a bronze man;

I was my body—with white stones

in my eye sockets, soldered veins in my wrists

and a delicately striated, crepelike scrotum.

Sighs, grunts, exhales, salt stains, dingy mats,

smeared mirrors and a faintly sour smell

filled the gulf between the mind and the world,

but the myth of love for another remained

bright and plausible, like an athlete painted

on the slope of a vase tying his sandal.

In the showers, tears fell from our hair,

as if from bent glistening sycamores.

It was as if Earth were taking us back.

6

In front of me, you are sleeping. I sleep also.

Probably you are right that I project

the ambiguities of my own desires.

I feel I only know you at the edges.

Sometimes in the night I jump up panting,

see my young gray head in the mirror

and fall back, as humans do, from the cold glass.

I don't have the time to invest in what

I purport to desire. But when you open

your eyes shyly and push me on the shoulder,

all I am is impulse and longing

pulled forward by the rope of your arm,

I, flesh-to-flesh, sating myself

on blurred odors of the soft black earth.

Acknowledgments

For their encouragement, I am indebted to the editors of the following publications, where poems, sometimes in different form, were originally published:

The American Poetry Review: "Ape House, Berlin Zoo," "Medusa," and "Powdered Milk." *The Atlantic Monthly*: "Black Camellia" and "Landscape with Deer and Figure." *Fence*: "Middle Earth." *Literary Imagination*: "Swans," "Melon and Insects," "Cleaning the Elephant," and "Veil." *The New England Review*: "Insomnia" and "Necessary and Impossible." *The New Republic*: "Mask," "Icarus Breathing," and "My Tea Ceremony." *The New Yorker*: "Self-Portrait in a Gold Kimono," "Casablanca Lily," "Myself with Cats," "Kyushu Hydrangea," "Pillowcase with Praying Mantis," "Radiant Ivory," and "Snow Moon Flower." *The Paris Review*: "At the Grave of Elizabeth Bishop." *Slate*: "Original Face" and "Crows in Evening Glow." *The Yale Review*: "The Hare" and "Fish and Watergrass." *Poems, Poets, Poetry* (edited by Helen Vendler): "Kayaks."

I would also like to record my thanks to the Japan–U.S. Friendship Commission for a Creative Artist Fellowship, which enabled me to live in the country of my birth during part of the composition of this book. My thanks also to the Bogliasco Foundation, the Corporation of Yaddo, and the American Academy in Berlin for hospitality and solitude during residencies.